EYEWITNESS ⦿ READERS

Level **2** AGES 6-8 YEARS

Firefighters

Written by Angela Royston

DK

DORLING KINDERSLEY
London • New York • Moscow • Sydney

One day Liz was checking the hoses to make sure they were screwed tightly to the fire engine. It is always busy at a fire station even when there is no fire.

A Note to Parents

Eyewitness Readers is a compelling new home reading programme for children. *Eyewitness* has become the most trusted name in illustrated books and this new series combines the highly visual *Eyewitness* approach with fun, easy-to-read stories. Each *Eyewitness Reader* is guaranteed to capture a child's interest while developing his or her reading skills, general knowledge and love of reading.

The books are written by leading children's authors and are designed in conjunction with literacy experts, including Cliff Moon M.Ed., Honorary Fellow of the University of Reading. Cliff Moon spent many years as a teacher and teacher educator specializing in reading. He has written more than 140 books for children and teachers and he reviews regularly for teachers' journals.

The four levels of *Eyewitness Readers* are aimed at different reading abilities, enabling you to choose the books that are exactly right for your child.
Level One for children aged three to six years
Level Two for children aged six to eight years
Level Three for children aged seven to nine years
Level Four for children aged eight to ten years

The "normal" age at which a child begins to read can be anywhere from three to eight years old, so these levels are intended only as a general guideline.

No matter which level you select, you can be sure that you're helping your child learn to read, then read to learn!

A Dorling Kindersley Book

Project Editor Lara Tankel Holtz
Art Editor Susan Calver
Senior Editor Linda Esposito
Deputy Managing Art Editor Jane Horne
Production Kate Oliver
Picture Reseasrch Jo Carlill
Photography Lynton Gardiner

Reading Consultant
Cliff Moon

Published in Great Britain by
Dorling Kindersley Limited
9 Henrietta Street
London WC2E 8PS

2 4 6 8 10 9 7 5 3 1

Visit us on the World Wide Web at http://www.dk.com

Eyewitness Readers™ is a trademark of
Dorling Kindersley Ltd.

Copyright © 1998 Dorling Kindersley Limited, London

A CIP catalogue record for this book is
available from the British Library

ISBN 0-7513-5771-5

Colour reproduction by Colourscan, Singapore
Printed and bound in Belgium by Proost

Special thanks to:
All the firefighters at Harrison Street Fire Station, New Rochelle
especially Danny Heinz, Anthony Costa, and Thomas Connell. All the
firefighters of Engine 24 and Hook & Ladder 5, New York City
John Santore of Hook & Ladder 5. Thank you also to Liz Radin.
The publisher would like to thank the following for their kind
permission to reproduce their photographs:
t=top, b=below, l=left, r=right, c=centre,
Colorific: Ian Bradshaw 23c; **Jim Pickerell** 12c; **Rex:** Cole 14tr;
Greg Williams 25c; **Tony Stone Images:** James McLoughlin 18c.
Colorific: P.F. Bently / Black Star front cover.

Dan was polishing
the wheels on
the fire engine.

Anthony was upstairs
in the kitchen,
looking for
a snack.
He is always
hungry!
Suddenly
a loud noise
made him jump.

Ring!
Ring!
Ring!

It was the fire alarm!
Anthony slid
down the pole.
THUD!
He landed hard.
But the thick
rubber pad
on the ground
cushioned his feet.

Liz jumped into her boots and pulled up her fireproof trousers. She checked the computer. It showed a fire at 7 Oak Lane. In the fire engine Liz grabbed the walkie-talkie. "Chief Miller! We're on our way!"

"Right!" said the
fire chief.
He had gone ahead
in a special fast car.
"I'll meet you there."

Liz started the engine
as the firefighters jumped in.
She flipped on the sirens and lights
and drove out of the fire station.
The truck rushed towards the fire.

All the cars and buses stopped and
waited when they heard the siren.

The fire chief called Liz.
"I'm at the scene of the fire.
It's an old house
that's been empty for years.
But someone saw a young boy
playing in the garden this morning.
He might be inside the house.
Tell Dan and Anthony to
get their air tanks ready."

"Okay, Chief," said Liz.
"I can see the smoke from here.
We'll be there in two minutes."

Liz turned the corner into Oak Lane.
Flames covered the top of the house.

The fire was spreading quickly.
There was no time to lose!

Hoses

Water comes out of a fire hose so fast it is strong enough to knock a person down.

Liz attached a hose from the engine to the nearest water hydrant.

A fire engine can pump water from a street hydrant to feed its hoses.

Liz and another firefighter pointed a hose at the flames.

"Ready!" called Liz.

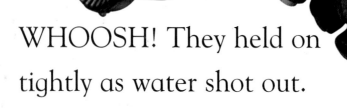

WHOOSH! They held on tightly as water shot out.

Breathing equipment
Fire gives off deadly smoke.
Firefighters wear air tanks
and breathing masks inside
a burning building.

Anthony and Dan got ready

to search the house.

They put on their

air tanks and face masks.

Each tank holds 40 minutes of air.

"The boy's name is Luke,"

the chief told them.

"You haven't got much time!"

"Right," said Anthony.

He grabbed a hose.

"Let's put the wet stuff

on the red stuff!" said Dan.

Dan and Anthony ran
to the back of the house.
The fire was not as bad there.
Dan felt the back door.
If it was hot, flames could leap out.
"It's cold," said Dan.
They stepped inside.

Thick black smoke was everywhere.
Anthony shone his torch around.
"Luke! Luke!" he called.
No one answered.
"I can hear fire upstairs," said Dan.
The fire had damaged the staircase.
It could fall down at any time.
They climbed the steps very carefully.

Outside, the stabilizers were set down on the ground.

Stabilizers are like legs.
They keep the truck steady
as the ladder is raised.
The ladder went up
like a telescope
to the top of the house.
A hose ran up the side.
The firefighter on the ladder
shot water down on to the fire.
The flames crackled and hissed.
They got smaller, then suddenly
jumped even higher.

Inside the house, the fire raged.
It was hot enough to melt glass.
Dan sprayed water on to the flames.
The fire had made the house weak.
"It could come down at any second,"
said Anthony. "We must find Luke."
BOOM!
A beam crashed down near them.
But their helmets protected their heads.
CRASH!
"Quick!" said Dan.
"We're running out of time."

Hard hats
Firefighters' helmets
are made of hard plastic.
A wide brim helps to keep
sparks off their necks.

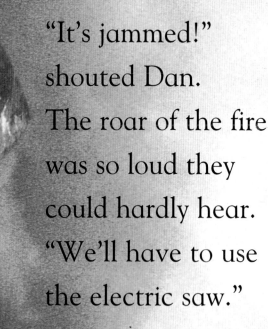

They came to another door.
But it would not open.
Dan swung his axe at the door.
Once. Twice. Three times.
"It's jammed!"
shouted Dan.
The roar of the fire
was so loud they
could hardly hear.
"We'll have to use
the electric saw."

Firefighter's axe
Axes have been
used by firefighters
since the earliest days
of firefighting.

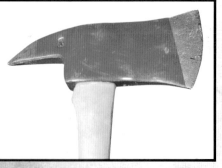

Sharp cutter
The electric saw
runs on batteries.
It can cut right through
the roof of a car
like a can opener.

Anthony switched on the saw.

WHIRRRR!

He cut a hole in the door,

big enough to climb through.

"Luke!" called Dan. "Luke?"

But the room was empty.

Suddenly the chief called. "Get out now! The roof is coming down!"

Dan and Anthony raced downstairs.
They got out just as the roof fell in.
"We didn't find Luke!" yelled Dan.
"He's okay," said the chief.
"We just found him up the road."
"Whew!" said Dan. "Good news!"

It took hours
to put out
all the flames.
Anthony sprayed
water on to
the parts still
glowing red.
He was tired
and dirty –
and very hungry!

Liz wound
the hoses back
on to the fire engine.
At last she could rest.
She felt worn out.

Back at the station
Anthony sat down to eat.
"At last!" he said.

Suddenly a loud noise
made him jump.
"Dinner will
have to wait!"
smiled Dan.

Ring!
Ring!
Ring!

Fire! What to do

- Leave the building immediately.

- If you can, close the door of the room where the fire is. This delays the spread of fire and smoke.

- Never open a closed door if it feels hot. Fire may be blazing on the other side.

- If you can't get out of the building, shut the door of the room you are in. Block any gaps with sheets or clothing. This will help to stop smoke coming in.

- If you are trapped in a smoke-filled room, crawl on the floor to a window. It's easier to breathe low down, because smoke rises.

- Open the window and shout for help.

- If you are in immediate danger, throw cushions or bedding to the ground to break your fall. Lower yourself out of the window to the full length of your arms before dropping.

- After you have got out of the building telephone the fire service on **999**.

Plan your escape route now.
Talk to your family about how you would get out of the house if there was a fire.

Dorling Kindersley would like to thank the Fire Safety
Division at the London Fire Brigade for their help.